FAN LING IN OCTO BER

Pui Ying Wong

Cover Design: Catherine Charbonneau
Calligraphy: Pui Ying Wong
Interior Design: Zoe Norvell

Published 2023 by Barrow Street, Inc.
(501) (c) (3) corporation. All contributions are tax deductible.
Distributed by:
    Barrow Street Books
    URI English Department, Swan 114
    60 Upper College Road
    Kingston, RI 02881

Barrow Street Books are also distributed by Small Press Distribution,
SPD, 1341 Seventh Street, Berkeley, CA 94710-1409, spd@spdbooks.
org; (510) 524-1668, (800) 869-7553 (Toll-free within the US); amazon.
com; Ingram Periodicals Inc., 1240 Heil Quaker Blvd, PO Box 7000,
La Vergne, TN 37086-700 (615) 213-3574; and Armadillo & Co., 7310
S. La Cienega Blvd, Inglewood, CA 90302, (310) 693-6061.

Special thanks to the University of Rhode Island English Department
and especially the PhD Program in English, 60 Upper College Road,
Swan 114, Kingston, RI 02881, (401) 874-5931, which provides
valuable in-kind support, including graduate and undergraduate interns.

First Edition

Library of Congress Control Number: 2023943283

ISBN: 978-1-962131-00-1

FANLING IN OCTOBER

PUI YING WONG

BARROW STREET PRESS
NEW YORK CITY

Contents

I.

Hotel Peninsula	1
Lamma Island	3
Be Water	5
Fanling in October	6
Day Tripping in Lau Fau Shan	8
A Gray of Light	9
Today, It	11
Between	12
Summer Last	13
Summer Ended Long Ago	14
Air Show	15
Bluing	16
In the City of Sirens	17
Winter Night	18
The Days After	19
River as Still Life	20
O	21
Night, the Wharf	22
Great Lawn, July	23
East River	24
A Morning Poem	25
A Tree Grows on the Stone Wall	26
On a Lovely Spring Day in the Park	28
Long Days and Cloudy	29
Sculpture Courtyard	31
Sunset over Amherst	32
Mount San Angelo	33
Bardigues	34

II.

Another Beginning   36

On the Quay Bercy   37

At the De Coligny Studio   39

August   40

Realism   41

Meng Chiao   42

Hotel Munchner Kindl   44

North Point Morning   45

Tu Fu's Tartar Horse   46

Memory of an Old Neighborhood   47

Day Optics   48

Near Crabapple Lane   49

The Walk   50

Night, Hospital   51

The Poem I Didn't   52

Of the Earth   53

Sugar High   54

With Them   55

Zen, Hunger   56

The Returning   57

New Year, Dawn   58

Night, Highway   60

Notes   61

Acknowledgments   62

About The Author   63

For Tim and Damon
and for my mother

Stars rise.
Moths flutter.
Apples sweeten in the dark.

—Eavan Boland

They are aware
that, on long journeys,
each bears the other,
whirring,
stirring
love occurring
in the middle of the terrifying air.

—James Baldwin

I.

Hotel Peninsula

Salisbury Road, Hong Kong

I know this place since childhood,
a baroque building with fancy boutiques
and an elegant café.

The fountain is the center piece,
a fleet of Rolls Royces
the backdrop.

It stands while the British
come and go.

It once housed Japanese occupiers
like Nazis in Paris did with The Ritz.

Nixon stayed here. So did Tom Cruise.

It faces the harbor named after an English Queen.
Sparkling hills and neon remind everyone
that the city was made by grit and money.

When an ocean liner comes in,
opulent like the Hall of Mirrors,
crowds rush to see it.

I find myself here after many years,
spotting the hotel from the ferry deck
and know

I have no use for its quaintness—
high tea and hush talks.

I miss the sampans,
their toughened, stitched-over sails,
their generations on board.

A grandmother might be at the steer,
a girl might be doing homework,
a way of life that would soon be gone
like a lost net.

I loved afternoons on the promenade
after escaping the stifling classroom,
my rebellion against rote learning, dead classics,
instructions given in a language not my own.

Some nights I watched ships
leaving the harbor and the future
grew in me like a sail.

I go after it. The sea is open.

Lamma Island

The dilapidated pier still holds a miracle,
winter light feeding it,
waves nip at its foot.

Bicycles ring their tiny bells, mixing in
with yells of *good morning*.

The locals talk of pork prices
and electricity, paying
no attention to the village loon
who's wailing in the loo.

We are here, tourists inconspicuous
as starfish.

In the hundred-year-old temple Tin Hou
looks out to the sea, unblinking.

We wander into the almost-new library,
a photograph exhibit
of fishing villages and kamikaze grottos.

These days there are more cargo boats
than fishing boats, more factory-dust
than monsoon.

A ferry away, the city is roiling.

Dioxide teargas, blue-dye water cannons
are daily occurrences, and
a university is under siege.

No one knows what comes next,
not even the young minister
leading prayers at last night's vigil.

Here the island is not god-loving
not empire-loving,
it loves itself

and no one needs a reminder
of the collision
that fateful evening,
the listed ferry,
the dead in the calm sea
and our return clocked for 5.

We pledge to come back soon
if the miracle doesn't count us out.

Be Water

—Hong Kong 2019

Bauhinias are bedraggled,
bruised.

The red of an empire spreads like jam
over every street.

The eye of the city looks back
at its own watermark,
twice colonized.

In the language of domination
what's changed is the way people
are regarded—

from *subjects* to *children*.

The bullet misses the boy's heart
by a fingernail.

People walk out into the heat
in mourning black,
trying to learn the way of water.

The eye of the city, thickened
by teargas, will not blink.

Fanling in October

My father in a hospital bed in a city
in which he's lived like an exile,
among bauhinia, thick air, hubbub and speed.
He's weak and to the therapists
who come to help he refuses.

He doesn't want to sit up.
He doesn't want to hold a spoon.
He doesn't want to open his eyes.

When he does see us, his children,
he roll-calls us
as if we are back from the missing.
The woman who is not our mother
feeds him congee. Everyone urges him to eat.

Eat, this tastes good.
Eat, you need strength.
Eat, so you can live (to ourselves)
The chorus sings heavily in the room.

Whatever we each think of
and what memories we keep
from one another submerge
like an underwater city.
He is no longer the young man who wrote:
the sun burns, flame of youth,
on a black-and-white photograph
he inscribed for my mother.
The photograph survives but not their love.

Nor is he the father I, as a girl, spotted from

the bedroom window,
coming home among commuters.
Head held high, back straight
like a man who thinks about pride.

If he has gone back he would see as I have,
that the bus terminal is gone,
the ferry is still there but not the fish venders
with their buckets of pikes and yellow croakers,
                              and where our home
once was, a new hotel,
gleaming like any other glass tower.

I think now about what's rent between us,
how a family dies not by knife or fire
but by drought, it's heart, shrinking,
                              so you wouldn't
notice at first.

Gradually the only conversations,
laughter and tears are those that pour out
from the television everyone stares at, eating dinner.
And when we finally disperse,
we disperse like nomads.
Like a nomad I leave behind things,
the window, the bed, jugs of sugar,
                              the cup I love drinking from.

Day Tripping in Lau Fau Shan

Shucked oysters
sleep in their wicker caskets

The fishmonger would like
to find a match
for her spinster daughter

Across the bay
Shenzhen the miracle
border city
ensnarls in factory haze

Get Rich is patriotic
even Mao's granddaughter
isn't hiding her billions

At the height of his power
Mao swam the width
of the Pearl River

And men escaping him
swam at night
with lights from the trawlers
Always a few
didn't make the journey

their bodies already blue
when washed up

A Gray of Light

Morning's headline—
amidst frantic political news the reporter finds
elegance in a preposition.

A lance of flags at rest like after-waves, adagio.

The republic is going down, the best of our optimists
says.

From the 19th floor rental studio I see
a headless cloud drifting off like a birthday cake
(without candles).

East of here the river and the suburbs,
north the rail roundabout one track out.
The phone buzzes.

No, I do not wish to share my location.

Behind the municipal building graffiti whispers,
I look and everyone is mad.

Though not the tourists, happily munching
on chocolate-filled cannoli.

Enthusiasm —god in you, Latin.

The optometrist I go to see has the enthusiasm
of a morgue attendant.

Like dogs we trace our markings:
We sat on that bench the first time.

Yes, we ate simple hotdogs there.

Poets gather moments like puddles gather rain.

Books on dystopia are in vogue.
Can the future still be read from oracle bones?

The invisible hands of God
are ever so light,
but he's still patrolling Eden.

Today, It

Today, it will be chrysanthemums.

Not hers or theirs but my grandfather's,
the ones he watered and pruned and sighed over
on a dismal day
                       —it's been half a century.
They shall lift from the clay of memory
into the cay of these lines.

Between

A crossed-out opening, on the other side: white,
between them so much life —Ryszard Krynicki

Between them so much life
and so much death

Is that why the crumpled paper burns
on both sides of the same shadow?

Summer Last

Days stretch like childhood,
like nylon socks.
Mosquitoes mate on the windows,
butterflies collapse on the road,
ice shifting in tumblers, mint juleps.
An open fire is banned,
no cigarettes, no barbecues.
Police copters circle overhead
like stalled plots, like ceiling fans,
and clock hands
turning out-of-time.
Talks of borders and wars,
talks of coming elections
and referendums, the peaceable
kingdom that never was.
Conversations continue
in check-out lines, at bus stops,
on the pixilated faces
of earphone wearers.
For fatigue and inattention
the doctor prescribes
sleep hygiene, for everyday
traumas in eyes and ears
there is no remedy.
No remedy for a blank notebook.
(But even nothing has to be written!)
Lines of geese fly off
like furrowed brows.
Grasses are all ears but the wind,
dying, can't tussle a single blade.

Summer Ended Long Ago

I was the woman going home
after a hard day.

I took the long way
across the soccer field,
no one was playing,
the clouds tasseled.

If there were still good things
in this world
I wanted to feel it in the ground
that holds me up,

catches me when I fall.

In my bag there was a head
of greens, salmon
from an island
buttressed by an old sea.

The sea said nothing. Nor could I.

Air Show

At 11 am six fighter jets ripped through
the sky. We were warned.
It was the British Royal Air Force
on tour, Boston, then New York…
Those who saw it said the whole thing
took seconds. A mass of red steel
hurled from nowhere, the air shook, then over.

Most of us stayed in the offices or gyms
like most mornings. It was sweltering already,
the sun ironed everything below.
A man's shirt clung to his back
like pain patches. Not too many people out,
at least not the old people in daycare
with nothing to do.

Bluing

The sky is blue, and bullets fly.
The sky is blue, and bullets fly.
The sky is blue, and bullets fly.
The sky is blue, and bullets fly.

Along a wild river and old villages,
Hung laundry and rubble,
Summer camp and freshwater, bullets fly.

The sky is blue, the sky is blue, the sky is blue.

In classrooms and in cinemas, in cafes
And in churches, in shopping malls and discos,
In barracks with flower beds and greenway, bullets fly,

Bullets fly, bullets fly, bullets fly.

In Sunday school amid bowed heads
And sacred texts, in parking lots
And on streets and highways, bullets fly.

Today, a man, a woman opens the door
To a blue sky, too blue,

The sky is blue.
The sky is blue.
The sky is blue.
The sky is blue.

In the City of Sirens

Friends have gone to join the activists' corps.
Some play cynics or with their cymbals of sounds.
Some leave for a new country all together.
The news is not good. There are many worlds to save.

We know evil walks on streets like ours, eats similar food.
It comes in garbs of sorts, even priests' and princes'.
Executioners practice their craft, barely bother with plots.
And our own, dead on city streets, slumped in cars.
Nothing is done. No one hears.

Poetry is useless like house keys with no address.
Some say let's start a honest conversation,
Forgetting that we've been talking and talking
Since the days of Homer.

So many houses on fire,
So many clouds, ringed with ash.

Winter Night

Wind picks up at midnight and puts
a shrill on our window.
The last walker and his dog
disappear quickly like specters.
Televisions replaying the president's
speech begin to dim, an afterglow
metastasized on the dark screens.
Thaw is nowhere,
the republic paralyzed like captives
in holding cells awaiting trials.
We doubt the almanac,
the misalignment of planets and stars.
We search history books but
they blow dust back at us.

The Days After

In November after America
voted,
no longer trusting the news—
wearied of petitions—
rueful in sleep—
forgetting birthdays and anniversaries
we went to poetry readings
hanging on every word,
ravenous like someone
in the midst of a bombed-out city
scavenging for bread.

River as Still Life

Today wine runs acid, no wind
rides on roses' perfume,
no light penetrates
this muck-green water. Beauty
can only get you so far,
the trail ahead is unknowable
as the day you first set forth.
You've heard the river answers
but words fret in your sachet,
odes you memorized
are useless as an appendix.

In the trees crows resume
their morning calls
and their songs, raw
as the newly bereaved
reach the solemn hour
when a great cathedral drowns.
You walk by casually
the world's spread of aperitif.
It is late. Toward upstream
you look, no sign of your dead
coming through.

O

On my desk a stack of stained papers
like Chinese joss paper
for the dead:
images inside stones,
unpassable lines,
strains of diversions and circuity,
answers that are questions,
questions that are orphaned,
not enough love, excessive,
reproach, doubt.

Words inflated, deflated,
murmurs and no-good fire,
promises and culs-de-sac,
void in forgetting,
a wounded arm finding
the elevator's buttons placed too high—
O my stillborn.

Night, the Wharf

Gradually lights go out from the beach houses.
The pier quiet as sleeping fish—
and the gulls, busy dropping
clams earlier, are gone too. The moon,
our faithful guide looks on,
vivid as a first memory.
Only the sea, after an exhaustive journey,
recedes, drawing a long breath
like someone who's arrived
at the destination, suddenly realizing
the return has started.

Great Lawn, July

We are on a bench, idling
like the poets we love.
A softball team goes home,
a young father pushes a pram,
two joggers compare numbers
on their wristwatches.
The air light like the instant
we left a crammed cinema
after seeing a heavy drama.

"Sit long enough, and
something arrives," a line
that is egoless,
whose author we forgot.
Dins of the day fade,
the world restores to peace.
Something comes back
like first love,
like hearing again the concert
once played in the fullness

of summer, altos
and altos—
Half-nodding, half-listening,
we sit like dinghies
in a no-wake zone,
finding what we lost,
losing what we found,
and neither one wants to leave
'til towers of lights arrive,
bright and owlish.

East River

The new ferries make
Circular runs

Old signs aglow
On the waterfront

Sugar-plant and Pepsi
-Cola plant   Dark

Warehouses are back
Making myths

Glass condos mirror
Lights and shadowing

Faces   the searchers'
Intense searching

A loud helicopter
On board the latest

Nouveau riche
Comes rather close

A shock of red
Like a lone

Strayed cardinal
Somewhere in the city a canyon

Hides humongous rocks
Of the once Ice Age

A Morning Poem

In a gothic-style writer's room
where I was a guest for a short stay,

there was nothing on the desk
other than an antiquated table lamp
and a rock the size of a fist.

And with a slightly flat body
and one pointy side it looked to me
like a miniature spaceship.

Rust-flecked and on its heels
it sat as a silent witness.

Outside, early morning fog
rolled past, dew gathered
in the grass, hush,

an occasional rumbling
of a distant train.

A Tree Grows on the Stone Wall

Something in the ground wouldn't
let it stay and sent a side
of the roots to the wall.

It may also be a case
of mutual aversion,
an impossible love.

A menacing passerby
would've nixed it
but didn't.

A squall should've ripped it,
a drought should've wilted it
and didn't.

It grows. In spite of.

It learns to love the wall
the way refugees learn to love
their host country.

It learns to take in rain,
nutrients through
secret channels.

Takes in all manner of lights,
from meager winter glare
to summer's harsh white heat.

All these take time. Then decades.

It is still learning.
Now it is to make one thing
only, a mural of it's own existence.

One decked with hairy roots,
inlaid with moss, ruby ash and liverwort.
No pedigree, alive with scars.

On a Lovely Spring Day in the Park

The teenage brother and sister approach me,
looking wholesome like breakfast cereal.

They hand me a note which reads:
Live Life to the Fullest.

I accept without quarrel, sooner or later
they'll learn the truth.

Long Days and Cloudy

Purification Day: rain sweeper.

The river's refusal to change course,
the windmill turning in one direction,
love's one track mind.

No one is a light unto himself
not even the sun.

Are you a poet only when you are writing?

No foxes in the snow. No snow,
a beggar-rooster crows.

When not writing poems
I pay bills,
study maps and check the weather.

Pour out sour milk, do laundry.

Diminished offering in love
is offensive. *If it has to be winter*
let it be absolutely winter.

Poems I didn't write are not the same
as the poems I couldn't write.

I still remember the bride,
her red dress swings against the time-
blasted façade of St. Severin.

Behind the heavy gate

a pagoda path, pure bliss even.
But no one is telling.

A gallery of ferns: grave sweeper.

Sculpture Courtyard

The sun came out and dried
the grass. I sat under a tree,
eating an apple. "Time to be healed"
the poet wrote. Stillness around me.
Language of metal and clay,
malleable as memory.
Cities were far.
Not much there I remembered.
September was only hinted at
by a few falling leaves.
Still, I didn't know about silence.
Silence between stars
and silence in time's deep caves.
I was like the coppery figure before me.
Earthbound, yet tilting
as if toward a great enigma.

Sunset over Amherst

An empty gazebo.
After dinner.

The sky turns,
kinks

of the day
smoothed.

Few paths converged
here,

one to the lake,
the other to the road,
one more to our studio.

Uneven patches of grass,
unknown berries,
ivies wild

around the bend.

The moon has a chip.
Pen scratches on paper.

Mount San Angelo

The hurricane misses it by twenty inches
of rain, but a slope of pussy willows
gets batted down.

Hidden from the road there is a scattering
of koi, safe in the pond, swimming
back and forth,
scarlet and gold.

Out on a walk from the hill we see
the residence, home for now.
Inside, artists are at work.

Come, my wayward muse,
untangle from your favorite
mummy suit.

This is the sound of fall. We must hurry.

Bardigues

By the river a sign warns
of sudden flooding
because of the nearby
nuclear power plant which looms
over tree farms and poppy fields.

Years back the utility company
built a new road and park,
giving out enticement like soldiers
do with candy bars
in occupied zones.

Now most townsfolk work there
and pray nothing bad happens.
We are in the next village,
one as pretty
as the guidebook says.

We sleep easily in a house
scented by a lush garden.
We too pray but sometimes
a squadron of black smoke escapes
into our dream and stays.

II.

Another Beginning

September light breaks on the boughs of trees,
birds fan out on the grass.
Once more the moment returns,
a moment that does not reject the world.
You are on a trail, studying its tricolor marks.
You travel light, mindful of stones and sticks.
Houses you left behind do not wait for you,
you are free
of lineage and club memberships.
You think not of countries but rivers, parks
and city streets, blue evenings
behind the bridge.
There's a parka in your rucksack for cold spells
(though there are winters you can never prepare for).
There's a book of poems about an immortal
swimming pool,
gore-tex and dog-eared, live and learn.
You think snow has no citizenship
and pain is not art. If a gaze
is as vast as love (as Paz envisioned)
it can hold the world and the world's wreckage.
At night when the stars spider out
you welcome your lawless dreams.
You are ready to believe the self
is at once forgettable and everything there is.
You are hardly the victim though you suffer.
September light breaks on the boughs of trees.

On the Quay Bercy

Sparrows under the table,
opera music from Petite Bain next door.
Fall in the air, wet rag of the hour,
trees holding tight their last strand of light.
Lady of Canton, I spotted the name
of the restaurant boat in Chinese characters.
Money-red, menstrual-red, red in a river of gray.
My language, my province, though truly,
mine was a castaway island.
I bought drinks from the African bartender,
flamboyant in his Panama hat, neck kerchief, taking
his time to impress the two sisters, and gesturing—
since everyone came with different languages,
the sweet in Mai Tai, the aftertaste of a double Triple Sec.
They sipped and swooned, would
one of them fall in love with him, or both?
The Seine flew before us, past this old
industrial winery, now new with outdoor cafes,
a swimming pool named after Josephine Baker.
They called her Black Pearl, Creole Goddess,
looking at her photographs I saw that radiance
and a woman who left home to find a country.
Rain scattered and returned, the river
ran toward other cities and towns,
known and little known canals and estuaries,
legends and myths. On the other side
large green buses plastered with discounted fares sped.
Disembarked passengers made their way
across the bridge, bags trailing.
I saw a young girl, her long hair tied up,
looking every which way for directions.
I was like her once, finding myself

on the verge of a strange city,
no home, no country to claim me,
in damp air and in dim light,
in mercy of the divine unknown.

At the De Coligny Studio

Vines have taken over
telephone poles and trees.
The barn with turrets and slated roofs,
stone paths to courtyards and rooms
recall the silhouette of a castle.
One I saw from my travel past
in some forgotten place,
forgotten years and seems only half-real.
                            Time from now
on a fast-moving train,
in markets bled of chatters,
what will my memory tell
of this room and its occupant.
A groundskeeper runs the mower.
A rabbit dashes and a turkey vulture,
as it is called by the locals,
high up, circles and circles.

August

For Constance Norgren

In an outer borough's
vacant lot,
a bush of moonflowers
furl in the daylight.

They are sensitive to
the sun,
flaring high on the towers.

Beats of a season
boiling over.

Wait for the moon to rise
and dark rims of turf emerge,

wait for the noise to die
and the bedtime milk taken,

for muscles around the constricted larynx
to relax.

Like the fragile voices of poets'
they will open

in fullness,
in August's cool shadows.

Realism

after *Snowy Fields* by Tom Keough

Snow lies in the foreground
in waves.

The curve line echoes
on the treetops,
and comes harder and tighter
like gathering clouds.

Between the dark
a path, lit by a volley of lights
so a night walker, if there
is one, can find her way.

On each side a bare birch,
the left one in shadows,
the one on the right is shone upon
in a rare hour of clarity.

The sky, barely visible,
conceals its drama for now.
With us are things to pass,

snow, birches, earthlights.

Meng Chiao

Perpetual wanderer poet
of dynasties past
is said to have never left his house
without writing a poem.

Years working in
some minor posts
must have made him weary
of the whims

of officials,
the pedigreed of courts
who wielded chicken feathers
at others like swords.

He journeyed on
through the drab of winter,
drag of wind,
came upon Loyang Town

once more
and wrote a series
of his famous Cold River poems.
Reading these poems

I can see that frozen world
hemmed in by thorns
on the shore
and the clanging sound

of the quartz-like river
still reverberates. He found

in every trail lost
many words for *sorrow*.

Hotel Munchner Kindl

The hostess has on a *Staten Island* shirt
and is not talkative
but says she likes New York.

The house breakfast serves
fresh farm eggs, lingonberry jam,
Tropicana juice if we want American.

Lace and velvet and a wingback chair,
the wall in our room a virgin green
out of the Black Forest.

My husband is in love with
the Bavarian beauty in the painting,
busty, slim-waist in a dirndl.

Octoberfest, a platoon of carriages
winds up and down *Tor Sendlinger.*
Flushed faces in the crowd, misted

from sleep, from longings. Horses
hold their head high, the cobbled streets
weep all afternoon the sound of their hooves.

North Point Morning

Sunrise on the Atlantic.
Birds untangle from trees,
houses coming into view, rail tracks,
sand and gravel, the blue depot.

The coyote is back
without his mate.
Last snow days you watched them
roaming the construction site, one
never far from the other.

(What happens happened
  out-of-sight).

By the look
of the leaves-choked yard
you sense a squall, like death,
swept through the night
and left.

And the strange woman
on Main Street,
cooing to her shopping cart
as if it was actually
a bassinet

is not so strange after all.

Tu Fu's Tartar Horse

after Mark Perlberg

Tu Fu gazes from his study,
war on his mind. Summer has gone
as have chattering rivers
and anglers' banters. The mountain,
grim-faced, receives daily lashes
of rain, even then, can't wash clean
the bits and burnt of the soldiers' fires.

Only by thinking of the horse,
her great frame and light hoofs
who can run ten thousand miles
in a fleeting morning,
who is heard of but unseen—
gives him peace
in a night long with an orphan moon.

Memory of an Old Neighborhood

Sunday Dinner, a Weekly Meal for the Hungry, a sign on
   the church door reads.

An elderly man hobbles on the sidewalk, trusting
   neither his aide nor the walker.

Letters arrive in my mailbox, get returned to sender.

I can't help anyone,
the door is jammed and won't open.

Day Optics

A wind turbine,
a dairy plant,
a new casino—rose gold
at the edge of water

Passersby on foot, on bikes, skates
and scooters
men hammering/sawing
men raking tar

A train halted by
the quay
a bridge lacing
into the next town

On the interstate cars crisscross
like the Milky Way
but it is only cataracts
seeing the whole world flown

Near Crabapple Lane

The mailbox raised
Its little red arm
The name Johnson
Written on the post
Behind the fence
Two or three dogs jump
Their barks reach
All the way to the hill
In the cemetery ground
Of the First Baptist Church
Where the headstone
Of Mr. J. Johnson
Is erected

The Walk

A row of trees
on a clear January day.
Winter has rendered

them leafless,
exposing their smooth trunks
and uncomplicated branches.

On my way to the station
I study their pattern,
a symmetry

in contrast to my own thoughts
which on this morning
are strands of formlessness.

The trees' presence
puts me at ease
but unlike friends, they ask

nothing of me,
not even a smile. It's more like
seeing a man's fate picked clean,

leaving him nothing to give
except a greeting in passing,
soft as a wisp of blue.

Night, Hospital

A thick glass separated us from the outside.

Snow slid down the roofs of the city,
windows ablaze with their own stars.

A book of poems on the dinner tray. You
in a cotton smock,

stained by vinegar.

The Poem I Didn't

The poem
I didn't
write
sits
like an old coin
in my coat
pocket one
I wear
winter-long
going cross-
town in early
evening
when the gold
of air
fall like nettings
and time
feels round
feels primitive I
rub my coin
to a shine
suddenly
the sun
slips
dark
is here

Of the Earth

Leave the window, let the bed
receive you like a simple lover.
Hear the small wind that tugs
at the curtain, the universe's soft arc.
Let childhood's lunar moon return, how
it trails after you like a loyal friend.
For so long you've gone from
here to there,

                      sometimes alone,
with others like a flotilla of stars.
You've learned one truth, you are worthy
of the earth's bitter roots. Sleep.
It's okay no one knows your sorrow
just as they don't know your joy.
Night still arrives for you, in splendor,
familiar as your own breath.

Sugar High

no more sugar at least no more than 10 grams
per day or 70 grams a week which equals
to 7 tablespoons mix in acid like a twist
of orange zest add flours eggs dashes
of baking soda for lift there comes
after 30 minutes in the oven
a sponge cake
buttery and golden—
no one says that's writing itself
but it's still something to look forward to
in our stay-at-home mode
no surprise I'm thinking of the madeleine
a bedbound Proust craves knowing
nothing lost can be returned whole
the longing doesn't stop the madness of it—
the head houses fortnight upon fortnight memory
long as a transcontinental train sober as a judge
all the days slow dancing on the white screen
my mouth laden with cake

With Them

once, in the dorm room,
I talked about life
like someone who doesn't know
about life

later, in the therapist's office,
I talked about death
like someone who doesn't know
about death

now,
I talk mostly of weather (since there's
a large window in my living room)

how insistent the rain, how the wind strikes
the trees to half mast

Zen, Hunger

Spring booms outside the window,
now forsythias, azaleas, cherry,
and no people.
Day by day grass runs rampant,
bogs fill.
Still no dogs, let alone sunbathers,
ballers or clowns.

                    We let it go,
let the season sling back to its skinny shed
like a lost groundhog.
No, we won't save an ant today,
nor a stray.
We slurp ramen noodles, wash it down
with schnapps, buck up for the night.

The Returning

Tired of sirens I rode a bus to the edge of town.
The streets were bare like it was a holiday.
I got off at the cemetery and went inside.
It was park-like with a stone tower and a lovely lake.
I walked along looping paths with names like lupine and thistle,
mimosa and cowslip, marigold and barberry.
It was as if I had entered a web of ancient tales,
the sky once more an elemental blue.
I no longer cared about the headlines,
the trauma and drowning and ambulance and knifing.
I sat on a rock near the water,
a stork skimming back and forth,
between frenzy and grace,
the endless returning one season after another.

New Year, Dawn

Clouds crawl above the houses,
chimera, unicorn, cat and mouse,
shape and shapeless, it is
whatever you want them to be.
Off they go flying without wings
into the vision of another insomniac
(deprived of sleep but may he
not be deprived of love)
who is biting his pencil hard
in a yellow-glowed room.
Time for resolutions, sunrise is coming.
I read a columnist's advice
"Willpower is for chumps"
just what I think I need more of.
The key, he goes on, is to cultivate
(does he mean coax?)
one's emotions to the task.
It sounds a little like an arranged marriage,
acts of love begetting love, and a little like religion,
acts of faith begetting faith.
And if this helps who is to argue?
But I rather think of one poet friend's
resolve, gold sweats ready to steel
against indifference, and another
who at midnight guards a tiny flame
like a mother bear. Poets know
their wounds can only be salved
by words.
Light wavers in this early hour, below me
a large construction site lays bare
its innards, cranes surround
it like a team of surgeons.

Maybe the patient is not past healing.
No tragedies have ever dislodged
a sunrise, call it the law of nature.
I make coffee for my husband.
We will drink it in the semi-dark
watch brightness return.
Scan today's headlines, eat breakfast,
call it habit, call it resiliency
which is a sort of love.

Night, Highway

I am on a long-distance bus, thinking
of the journey ahead.
Lights peer from the dark woods,
faint TV images.
In the air comes the scent of burning logs,
scent of a place where I am absent.
Memory's door suddenly opens,
allowing glimpses of a lost world.
Some shreds of clouds, a hill,
houses and a garden lit by green lanterns.
And the girl that I was remains there
running her heart out, but whereto
and what was the message
I can't say, even now.
Outside, the sky is close as a whisper,
the flattened landscape seems
to squeeze out time. Strapped
to my seat I lean forward, moments
swirl past once more like hisses of fire.

Notes

Hotel Peninsula
The Peninsula Hong Kong was built in 1924 in Tsim Sha Tsui, Kowloon, a location directly facing Victoria Harbor. A luxury hotel, it was used by the Japanese military as their headquarters when they occupied the city during WWII. The building's architecture reflects Hong Kong's colonial past.

Lamma Island
Lamma, one of the hundreds of outlying islands, is reachable by a half-hour ferry ride from Hong Kong.

Be Water
Be Water was a term adopted by the Hong Kong protestors during the 2019 democracy movement. The tactics include constantly moving around to various neighborhoods in order to evade and dilute the police force. It was a martial arts term originally used by the actor and Hong Kong icon Bruce Lee to suggest fluidity in dealing with opposition.

Fanling in October
Fanling is a northern suburb of Hong Kong. It used to be clusters of small farming villages until development in the 1980s brought in massive housing blocks.

Day Tripping in Lau Fau Shan
Lau Fau Shan is an area in New Territories known for oyster farms. From there, Shenzhen, the southern city in mainland China is visible on the other side of the bay.

Long Days and Cloudy
The third stanza includes a quote by Antonio Porchia; the eighth stanza quotes Linda Gregg.

Acknowledgments

Grateful acknowledgment is made to editors of the following publications in which these poems first appeared:

Blue Mountain Review, Blue Nib, Chautauqua Review, Cider Press, Connecticut River Review, Constellations, Dillydoun Review, Foliate Oak, Hamilton Stone Review, Hanging Loose, Hotel Amerika, Looking Back At Hong Kong—An Anthology of Writing and Art, Lyrical Somerville, Mercurius, Mojave River Review, Muddy River Review, New Letters, New World Writing, Penn Review, Pensive Journal, Streetlight Magazine, Sublunary Review, SWWIM, Unlikely Stories Mark V, Visitant, Word City, Zone 3.

Deep thanks to Rachel Rothenberg, Sharon Dolin, Shannon Carson and everyone at Barrow Street Press for their wonderful support.

PUI YING WONG is the author of three full-length books of poetry, *The Feast, An Emigrant's Winter* and *Yellow Plum Season*, along with two chapbooks, *Mementos* and *Sonnet for a New Country*. She has received a Pushcart Prize. Her poems have appeared in *Ploughshares, Plume, Prairie Schooner, The Southampton Review, Chicago Quarterly Review*, among many others. Born and raised in Hong Kong, she lives in Cambridge, Massachusetts with her husband, the poet Tim Suermondt.

BARROW STREET POETRY

Close Red Water
Emma Aylor 2023

Landscape with Missing River
Joni Wallace 2023

Down Low and Lowdown...
Timothy Liu 2023

the archive is all
in present tense
Elizabeth Hoover 2022

Person, Perceived Girl
A.A. Vincent 2022

Frank Dark
Stephen Massimilla 2022

Liar
Jessica Cuello 2021

On the Verge of Something Bright
and Good
Derek Pollard 2021

The Little Book of
No Consolation
Becka Mara McKay 2021

Shoreditch
Miguel Murphy 2021

Hey Y'all Watch This
Chris Hayes 2020

Uses of My Body
Simone Savannah 2020

Vortex Street
Page Hill Starzinger 2020

Exorcism Lessons
in the Heartland
Cara Dees 2019

American Selfie
Curtis Bauer 2019

Hold Sway
Sally Ball 2019

Green Target
Tina Barr 2018

Luminous Debris: New &
Selected Legerdemain
Timothy Liu 2018

We Step into the Sea: New
and Selected Poems
Claudia Keelan 2018

Adorable Airport
Jacqueline Lyons 2018

Whiskey, X-ray, Yankee
Dara-Lyn Shrager 2018

For the Fire from the Straw
Heidi Lynn Nilsson 2017

Alma Almanac
Sarah Ann Winn 2017

A Dangling House
Maeve Kinkead 2017

Noon until Night
Richard Hoffman 2017

Kingdom Come Radio Show
Joni Wallace 2016

In Which I Play the Run Away
Rochelle Hurt 2016

*The Dear Remote
Nearness of You*
Danielle Legros Georges 2016

Detainee
Miguel Murphy 2016

*Our Emotions Get Carried Away
Beyond Us*
Danielle Cadena Deulen 2015

Radioland
Lesley Wheeler 2015

Tributary
Kevin McLellan 2015

Horse Medicine
Doug Anderson 2015

This Version of Earth
Soraya Shalforoosh 2014

Unions
Alfred Corn 2014

O, Heart
Claudia Keelan 2014

Last Psalm at Sea Level
Meg Day 2014

Vestigial
Page Hill Starzinger 2013

*You Have to Laugh:
New + Selected Poems*
Mairéad Byrne 2013

Wreck Me
Sally Ball 2013

*Blight, Blight, Blight,
Ray of Hope*
Frank Montesonti 2012

Self-evident
Scott Hightower 2012

Emblem
Richard Hoffman 2011

Mechanical Fireflies
Doug Ramspeck 2011

Warranty in Zulu
Matthew Gavin Frank 2010

Heterotopia
Lesley Wheeler 2010

This Noisy Egg
Nicole Walker 2010

Black Leapt In
Chris Forhan 2009

Boy with Flowers
Ely Shipley 2008

Gold Star Road
Richard Hoffman 2007

Hidden Sequel
Stan Sanvel Rubin 2006

Annus Mirabilis
Sally Ball 2005

A Hat on the Bed
Christine Scanlon 2004

Hiatus
Evelyn Reilly 2004

3.14159+
Lois Hirshkowitz 2004

Selah
Joshua Corey 2003